The A
Transformed a Nation

Lessons from the Great Awakening
of the Eighteenth Century

J. C. Ryle

Foreword

For many years J. C. Ryle's *Christian Leaders of the 18th Century* has been in my list of top ten books that I urge all Christians to read. This particular introductory chapter is one we often study when small groups go away on a reading party. It is very encouraging because it reminds us that there was a time when things in our nation were even worse than they are now; but God graciously intervened and brought about a remarkable change. It is also a very challenging read because it teaches us that God did this through faithful men, who worked very hard as they preached the gospel and taught the Bible. Yet there was no grand scheme or planned strategy. What was significant and important was faithful Bible ministry. The need of the hour in this twenty-first century is equally urgent. This must be the way ahead for us today. It is great news that this chapter is being reproduced and made accessible in this format.

Rev Jonathan Fletcher
Emmanuel Church,
Wimbledon

Introduction

IN 1885 J. C. Ryle published his book, *Christian Leaders of the 18th Century*. It was a compilation of what had been a series of articles in a monthly magazine called *The Family Treasury*. *Christian Leaders* is still in print today and is published by the Banner of Truth Trust.

Most of the volume comprises ten biographies of 18th-century evangelists in Great Britain, men such as Wesley and Whitefield, Grimshaw and Berridge. To read of these men is to be abundantly blessed, and I would plead with you to do so. Ryle was a minister of the Church of England, and later became the first Bishop of Liverpool, so we can surely forgive him for the small amount of bias in his writings towards his beloved Church of England.

Before introducing us to the life and work of these Christian leaders, Ryle paints a picture of the dire spiritual and moral state of the land in the 18th century and its impact on the economic and educational conditions of England and Wales. There was great spiritual darkness before the dawn and brightness of a new day.

This booklet is a reproduction of chapter two of Ryle's book. The author entitled the chapter, 'The Agency by which Christianity was Revived in England.' It is fascinating because of its relevance to our situation today. I hope it will be read, not so much as an historical treatise, but as a handbook for all of us who want to see the good news of the Lord Jesus Christ make an impact on our land. Every time I have read it, I have been fired and enthused to make Christ crucified known to all. It was a catalyst for me to write the book, *And Some Evangelists*, in which I encourage churches to identify, use and set aside evangelists for such an important work. Now I pray that nearly one hundred and fifty years since Ryle first wrote these words, God will use them to instruct, enthuse, and bless you too, to the glory of God alone.

Roger Carswell

The Agency that Transformed a Nation

THAT a great change for the better has come over England in the last hundred years[1] is a fact which I suppose no well-informed person would ever attempt to deny. You might as well attempt to deny that there was a Protestant Reformation in the days of Luther, a Long Parliament in the time of Cromwell, or a French Republic at the end of the eighteenth century. There has been a vast change for the better. Both in religion and morality the country has gone through a complete revolution. People neither think, nor talk, nor act as they did in 1750. It is a great fact, which the children of this world cannot deny, however they may attempt to explain it. They might as well try to persuade us that high-water and low-water at London Bridge are one and the same thing.

But by what agency was this great change effected? To whom are we indebted for the immense improvement in

[1] Ryle originally wrote these words in 1868, and so is referring to the period from around the middle of the eighteenth century.

religion and morality which undoubtedly has come over the land? Who, in a word, were the instruments that God employed in bringing about the great English reformation of the eighteenth century?

This is the one point that I wish to examine generally in this booklet. The names and biographies of the principal agents may be found elsewhere.[2]

The government of the country can lay no claim to the credit of the change. Morality cannot be called into being by penal enactments and statutes. People were never yet made religious by Acts of Parliament. At any rate, the Parliaments and administrations of the eighteenth century did as little for religion and morality as any that ever existed in England.

Nor yet did the change come from the Church of England, as a body. The leaders of that venerable communion were utterly unequal to the times. Left to herself, the Church of England would probably have died of dignity, and sunk at her anchors.

Nor yet did the change come from the Dissenters. Content with their hardly-won triumphs, that worthy body of men seemed to rest upon their oars. In the plenary enjoyment of their rights of conscience, they forgot the great vital principles of their forefathers, and their

---

[2] See Ryle's book, *Christian Leaders of the 18th Century,* reprinted by the Trust.

own duties and responsibilities.

Who, then, were the reformers of the eighteenth century? To whom are we indebted, under God, for the change which took place? The men who wrought deliverance for us, all those years ago, were a few individuals, most of them clergymen of the Established Church, whose hearts God touched about the same time in various parts of the country. They were not wealthy or highly connected. They had neither money to buy adherents, nor family influence to command attention and respect. They were not put forward by any Church, party, society, or institution. They were simply men whom God stirred up and brought out to do his work, without previous concert, scheme, or plan. They did his work in the old apostolic way, by becoming the evangelists of their day. They taught one set of truths. They taught them in the same way, with fire, reality, earnestness, as men fully convinced of what they taught. They taught them in the same spirit, always loving, compassionate, and, like Paul, even weeping, but always bold, unflinching, and not fearing the face of man. And they taught them on the same plan, always acting on the aggressive; not waiting for sinners to come to them, but going after, and seeking sinners; not sitting idle till sinners offered to repent, but assaulting the high places of ungodliness like men storming a breach, and giving sinners no rest so long as they stuck to their sins.

The movement of these gallant evangelists shook England from one end to another. At first people in high places affected to despise them. The men of letters sneered at them as fanatics; the wits cut jokes, and invented smart names for them; the Church shut her doors on them; the Dissenters turned the cold shoulder on them; the ignorant mob persecuted them. But the movement of these few evangelists went on, and made itself felt in every part of the land. Many were aroused and awakened to think about religion; many were shamed out of their sins; many were restrained and frightened at their own ungodliness; many were gathered together and induced to profess a decided hearty religion; many were converted; many who affected to dislike the movement were secretly provoked to emulation. The little sapling became a strong tree; the little rill became a deep, broad stream; the little spark became a steady burning flame. A candle was lighted, of which we are enjoying the benefit. The feeling of all classes in the land about religion and morality gradually assumed a totally different complexion. And all this, under God, was effected by a few unpatronized, unpaid adventurers! When God takes a work in hand, nothing can stop it. When God is for us, none can be against us.

The instrumentality of preaching

The instrumentality by which the spiritual reformers of the eighteenth century carried on their operations was of the simplest description. It was neither more nor less than the old apostolic weapon of *preaching*. The sword which St Paul wielded with such mighty effect, when he assaulted the strongholds of heathenism in the first century, was the same sword by which they won their victories. To say, as some have done, that they neglected education and schools, is totally incorrect. Wherever they gathered congregations, they cared for the children. To say, as others have done, that they neglected the sacraments, is simply false. Those who make that assertion only expose their entire ignorance of the religious history of England in the eighteenth century. It would be easy to name men among the leading reformers of that period whose communicants might be reckoned by hundreds, and who honoured the Lord's Supper more than forty-nine out of fifty clergymen in their day. But beyond doubt preaching was their favourite weapon. They wisely went back to first principles, and took up apostolic plans. They held, with St Paul, that a minister's first work is 'to preach the gospel'.

They preached *everywhere*. If the pulpit of a parish church was open to them, they gladly availed themselves of it. If it could not be obtained, they were equally ready to preach in a barn. No place came amiss to them. In the field or by the road-side, on the village-green or in a market-place, in lanes or in alleys, in cellars or in garrets, on a tub or on a table, on a bench or on a horse-block, wherever hearers could be gathered, the spiritual reformers of the eighteenth century were ready to speak to them about their souls. They were instant in season and out of season in doing the fisherman's work, and compassed sea and land in carrying forward their Father's business. Now, all this was a new thing. Can we wonder that it produced a great effect?

They preached *simply*. They rightly concluded that the very first qualification to be aimed at in a sermon is to be understood. They saw clearly that thousands of able and well-composed sermons are utterly useless, because they are above the heads of the hearers. They strove to come down to the level of the people, and to speak what the poor could understand. To attain this they were not ashamed to crucify their style, and to sacrifice their reputation for learning. To attain this they used illustrations and anecdotes in abundance, and, like their divine Master, borrowed lessons from every object in nature. They carried out the maxim of Augustine, — 'A wooden key is not so beautiful as a golden one, but if it can open the door when the golden one cannot, it is far more useful.' They revived the style of sermons in which Luther and Latimer used to be so eminently successful. In short, they saw the truth of what the great German reformer meant when he said, 'No one can be a good preacher to the people who is not willing to preach in a manner that seems childish and vulgar to some.' Now, all this again was quite new in the eighteenth century.

They preached *fervently and directly*. They cast aside that dull, cold, heavy, lifeless mode of delivery, which had long made sermons a very proverb for dullness. They proclaimed the words of the faith with faith, and the story of life with life. They spoke with fiery zeal, like men who were thoroughly persuaded that what they said was true, and that it was of the utmost importance to your eternal interest to hear it. They spoke like men who had got a message from God to you, and must deliver it, and have your attention while they delivered it. They threw heart, soul and feeling into their sermons, and sent their hearers home convinced, at any rate, that the preacher was sincere and wished them well. They believed that you must speak *from* the heart if you wish to speak *to* the heart, and that there must be unmistakable faith and conviction within the pulpit if there is to be faith and conviction among the pews. All this, I repeat, was a thing that had become almost obsolete in the eighteenth century. Can we wonder that it took people by storm, and produced an immense effect?

The substance of their preaching

But what was the substance and subject-matter of the preaching which produced such wonderful effect in those days?

I will not insult my readers' common sense by only saying that it was 'simple, earnest, fervent, real, genial, brave, life-like', and so forth; I would have it understood that it was eminently doctrinal, positive, dogmatical, and distinct. The strongholds of the sins of the eighteenth century would never have been cast down by mere earnestness and negative teaching. The trumpets which blew down the walls of Jericho were trumpets which gave no uncertain sound. The English evangelists of that period were not men of an uncertain creed. But what was it that they proclaimed? A little information on this point may not be without use.

For one thing, then, the spiritual reformers of the eighteenth century taught constantly *the sufficiency and supremacy of Holy Scripture*. The Bible, whole and unmutilated, was their sole rule of faith and practice. They accepted all its statements without question or dispute. They knew nothing of any part of Scripture being uninspired. They never allowed that man has any 'verifying faculty' within him, by which Scripture statements may be weighed, rejected, or received. They never flinched from asserting that there can be no error in the Word of

God; and that when we cannot understand or reconcile some part of its contents, the fault is in the interpreter and not in the text. In all their preaching they were eminently men of one book. To that book they were content to pin their faith, and by it to stand or fall. This was one grand characteristic of their preaching, They honoured, they loved, they reverenced the Bible.

Furthermore, these reformers taught constantly the *total corruption of human nature*. They knew nothing of the modern notion that Christ is in every man, and that all possess something good within, which they have only to stir up and use in order to be saved. They never flattered men and women in this fashion. They told them plainly that they were dead, and must be made alive again; that they were guilty, lost, helpless, and hopeless, and in imminent danger of eternal ruin. Strange and paradoxical as it may seem to some, their first step towards making men good was to show them that they were utterly bad; and their primary argument in persuading men to do something for their souls was to convince them that they could do nothing at all.

Furthermore, the reformers of the eighteenth century taught constantly that *Christ's death upon the cross was the only satisfaction for man's sin*; and that when Christ died, he died as our substitute — 'the just for the unjust'. This, in fact, was the cardinal point in almost all their sermons. They never taught the modern doctrine that Christ's death was only a great example of self-sacrifice. They saw in it something far higher, greater, deeper than this. They saw in it the payment of man's mighty debt to God. They loved Christ's person; they rejoiced in Christ's promises; they urged men to walk after Christ's example. But the one subject, above all others, concerning Christ, which they delighted to dwell on, was the atoning blood which Christ shed for us on the cross.

Furthermore, the reformers of the eighteenth century taught constantly *the great doctrine of justification by faith*. They told men that faith was the one thing needful in order to obtain an interest in Christ's work for their souls; that before we believe, we are dead, and have no interest in Christ; and that the moment we do believe, we live, and have a plenary title to all Christ's benefits. Justification by virtue of church membership — justification without believing or trusting — were notions to which they gave no countenance. Everything, if you will believe, and the moment you believe; nothing, if you do not believe, — was the very marrow of their preaching.

Furthermore, the reformers of the eighteenth century taught constantly the *universal necessity* of heart conversion and a new creation by the Holy Spirit. They proclaimed everywhere to the crowds whom they addressed, 'Ye must be born again.' Sonship to God by baptism — sonship to God while we do the will of the devil — such sonship they never admitted. The regeneration which they preached was no dormant, torpid, motionless thing. It was something that could be seen, discerned, and known by its effects.

Furthermore, the reformers of the eighteenth century taught constantly the *inseparable connection between true faith and personal holiness.* They never allowed for a moment that any church membership or religious profession was the least proof of a man being a true Christian if he lived an ungodly life. A true Christian, they maintained, must always be known by his fruits; and these fruits must be plainly manifest and unmistakable in all the relations of life. 'No fruits, no grace', was the unvarying tenor of their preaching.

Finally, the reformers of the eighteenth century taught constantly, as doctrines both equally true, *God's eternal hatred against sin*, and *God's love towards sinners*. They knew nothing of a 'love lower than hell', and a heaven where holy and unholy are all at length to find admission. Both about heaven and hell they used the utmost plainness of speech. They never shrank from declaring, in plainest terms, the certainty of God's judgment and of wrath to come, if men persisted in impenitence and unbelief; and yet they never ceased to magnify the riches of God's kindness and compassion, and to entreat all sinners to repent and turn to God before it was too late.

Such were the main truths which the English evangelists of the eighteenth century were constantly preaching. These were the principal doctrines which they were always proclaiming, whether in town or in country, whether in church or in the open air, whether among rich or among poor. These were the doctrines by which they turned England upside down, made ploughmen and colliers weep till their dirty faces were seamed with tears, arrested the attention of peers and philosophers, stormed the strongholds of Satan, plucked thousands like brands from the burning, and altered the character of the age. Call them simple and elementary doctrines if you will. Say, if you please, that you see nothing grand, striking, new, peculiar about this list of truths. But the fact is undeniable, that God blessed these truths to the reformation of England in the eighteenth century. What God has blessed it ill becomes man to despise.